THE RETURN OF THE GREEN SEA TURTLE

MELISSA RAÉ SHOFNER

PowerKiDS press.

New York

Published in 2018 by The Rosen Publishing Group, Inc.
29 East 21st Street, New York, NY 10010

First Edition

Editor: Theresa Morlock
Book Design: Reann Nye

Photo Credits: Cover Lotus41/Moment/Getty Images; p. 4 dive-hive/Shutterstock.com; p. 5 (Pyrenean ibex) dragoms/Moment Open/Getty Images; p. 5 (jaguar) Travel Stock/Shutterstock.com; p. 5 (Arctic fox, hippopotamus) bikeriderlondon/Shutterstock.com; p. 5 (orangutan) Uryadnikov/Shutterstock.com; p. 5 (Wyoming toad) https://commons.wikimedia.org/wiki/File:Bufo_baxteri-3.jpg; p. 6 idreamphoto/Shutterstock.com; p. 7 pingebat/Shutterstock.com; p. 9 Daniel Wilhelm Nilsson/Shutterstock.com; p. 10 JonMilnes/Shutterstock.com; p. 11 Matt Oldfield-Scubazoo/Science Faction/Getty Images; p. 12 DJ Mattaar/Shutterstock.com; p. 13 Rich Carey/Shutterstock.com; p. 14 Levent Konuk/Shutterstock.com; p. 15 Amanda Nicholls/Shutterstock.com; p. 16 Danny E Hooks/Shutterstock.com; p. 17 Sergi Garcia Fernandez/Biosphoto/Getty Images; p. 19 David Evison/Shutterstock.com; p. 20 Jurgen Freund/Nature Picture Library/Getty Images; p. 21 FamVeld/Shutterstock.com; p. 22 Greg Amptman/Shutterstock.com; p. 23 mai111/Shutterstock.com; p. 25 Pete Oxford/Minden Pictures/Getty Images; p. 26 Bonita R. Cheshier/Shutterstock.com; p. 27 tropicdreams/Shutterstock.com; p. 28 KidStock/Blend Images/Getty Images; p. 29 apiguide/Shutterstock.com; p. 30 Isabelle Kuehn/Shutterstock.com.

Library of Congress Cataloging-in-Publication Data

Names: Shofner, Melissa Raé, author.
Title: The return of the green sea turtle / Melissa Raé Shofner.
Description: New York : PowerKids Press, [2018] | Series: Bouncing back from extinction | Includes index.
Identifiers: LCCN 2017013080| ISBN 9781508156246 (pbk. book) | ISBN 9781508156055 (6 pack) | ISBN 9781508156178 (library bound book)
Subjects: LCSH: Green turtle–Juvenile literature.
Classification: LCC QL666.C536 S56 2018 | DDC 597.92/8–dc23
LC record available at https://lccn.loc.gov/2017013080

Manufactured in the United States of America

CPSIA Compliance Information: Batch #BS17PK: For Further Information contact Rosen Publishing, New York, New York at 1-800-237-9932

CONTENTS

GIANTS OF THE SEA

Green sea turtles are some of the most amazing creatures in our planet's oceans. These gentle giants are known for swimming long distances back and forth between their feeding and nesting areas. They've played an important role in keeping the oceans healthy for millions of years. Unfortunately, humans have hurt green sea turtle populations more and more over the past several centuries.

Today, green sea turtles are considered endangered in many places. Scientists don't have much information about how many green sea turtles were on Earth when their populations first began to **decline**, but it's clear there are fewer alive now than there were in the past, and their populations continue to suffer. In order to save green sea turtles, we must first understand how we harm them.

Humans and green sea turtles—also called green turtles or greens—have had a troubled past. Today, many people are working hard to save these beautiful animals.

CONSERVATION STATUS CHART

EXTINCT

Having no living members.

Pyrenean ibex

EXTINCT IN THE WILD

Living members only in captivity.

Wyoming toad

CRITICALLY ENDANGERED

At highest risk of becoming extinct.

Sumatran orangutan

ENDANGERED VULNERABLE

High risk of extinction in the wild.

hippopotamus

NEAR THREATENED

Likely to become endangered soon.

jaguar

LEAST CONCERN

Lowest risk of endangerment.

Arctic fox

GREEN TURTLE FACTS

Despite their name, green sea turtles aren't usually green. Their shell may be brown, yellow, gray, or even black. Their name actually comes from a layer of green fat beneath their shell. This green coloring is thought to come from the sea grass and **algae** they eat.

Greens are the second-largest type of sea turtle. On average they weigh around 350 pounds (158.8 kg)

GREEN SEA TURTLES OF HAWAII

There's a population of green sea turtles that never leaves the area around the Hawaiian Islands. Scientists don't think they breed with other greens outside this population. They're also the only greens known to come on shore outside of the breeding season.

GREEN SEA TURTLE HABITAT

| nest site | coastal home range |

| migration range |

North America

Europe

Asia

Africa

South America

Australia

This map shows where green sea turtles live, migrate, and nest. Nesting beaches are found in more than 80 countries around the world.

and can grow up to 4 feet (1.2 m) long. These reptiles spend much of their time in warm, shallow coastal waters. During breeding season, they'll often swim long distances across the open ocean to nesting sites. This is called migration. For most greens, nesting is the only time they'll leave the water and come on shore.

HISTORY WITH HUMANS

Sea turtles have lived on Earth for more than 100 million years. During this time, they've been able to successfully adapt and survive. Over the past few centuries, however, green turtle populations have greatly declined, largely due to people.

Throughout history, green sea turtles have been important to many native peoples in the Pacific islands. In some societies, the use of turtles was controlled by a council or chief. Green turtles provided meat and eggs to eat, and their bones and shells were made into tools, jewelry, and other objects. Their fat was also used to treat burns and various skin problems. In the Hawaiian Islands, some families protected green sea turtles. They believed the green turtle was a family deity, or god.

TURTLE EXCLUDER DEVICES

Each year, thousands of sea turtles drown after being accidentally caught in shrimp nets. In 1992, the United States passed a law that required all U.S. shrimp boats to use special turtle **excluder** devices (TEDs) while working in areas where sea turtles are known to live. These devices attach to fishing nets and allow turtles to escape while keeping shrimp inside the net.

Green sea turtles continue to be important to some cultures in the Pacific today.

In the 1500s, European explorers in Central America encountered green sea turtles for the first time. Many populations were hunted to near extinction as explorers began killing the turtles for their meat, shell, skin, and eggs. These goods were sometimes sent back to Europe, and the turtle trade began.

International trade of sea turtles would continue for hundreds of years. In the 1970s, hundreds of thousands

Today, poaching, or illegal hunting, of green turtles remains a big problem in many places. In some places, turtle hunting is legal.

of turtles were killed each year for a variety of uses. The Sea Turtle Conservation Strategy of 1979 noted that sea turtles "have been **overexploited** most frequently to feed, clothe, and **adorn** the wealthy in Europe, North America, and eastern Asia." Despite tough laws placed on the international turtle trade in the 1970s and 1980s, these practices continue to harm turtle populations today.

UNDERWATER GARDENERS

When green sea turtles are young, they're omnivores. Jellyfish are one of their favorite foods. As they grow older, their diet changes. Adult greens are the only sea turtles that are herbivores.

Greens are some of the only animals that eat sea grass. They play an important role in the **ecosystem** by keeping the sea grass trimmed, which keeps it healthy. Untrimmed sea grass becomes unhealthy and dies. In the

ECOLOGICAL EXTINCTION

If green sea turtle populations continue to decline, it may lead to their ecological extinction. A species is considered ecologically extinct when it doesn't have enough individuals to properly perform its role in an ecosystem. This may eventually cause an ecosystem to collapse.

Green sea turtles have serrated, or sawlike, jaws that are perfect for chewing through sea grass.

last few decades, there has been a noticeable loss of sea grass. Scientists think this may be because there are fewer sea turtles.

All the plants and animals within an ecosystem depend on each other to survive. Sea grass provides homes, hiding places, and breeding areas for many types of sea creatures. Without green sea turtles to maintain the sea grass, many ocean species will suffer.

LONG LIVES

Green sea turtles have very long lives. Scientists believe they may be able to live for 80 years or more in the wild. You might think there would be many greens in the sea since they live so long, but there are many things working against them.

It's hard for green sea turtles to grow their populations because they can't have offspring, or babies, until they're between 20 and 50 years old. A lot can

Scientists have a difficult time estimating the population size of green sea turtles in the wild. There's still much to learn about these animals' long lives.

happen to a turtle between the time it hatches and when it's old enough to have offspring of its own. In fact, scientists believe that only 1 in 1,000 green sea turtles will survive into adulthood. Greens that do make it to adulthood must then deal with issues related to their migrations and nesting sites.

GLOBAL WARMING AND POLLUTION

When people burn fuels such as coal, greenhouse gases are released. These gases are causing Earth's temperature to increase over time. This is called global warming, and it's hurting green turtle populations.

The temperature of the sand around green turtle eggs determines if baby turtles, called hatchlings, will be male or female. Higher temperatures lead to more females. Warmer sand caused by global warming is

DIFFERENT TYPES OF DISASTERS

Natural **disasters** such as hurricanes sometimes damage nesting sites. Strong winds and waves can erode, or wear away, beaches and destroy nests. **Environmental** disasters such as oil spills are also huge problems. Oil doesn't usually stick to green turtles like it does to other marine animals. However, greens may eat tar balls floating in the ocean after a spill, which can hurt their insides.

Trash in the oceans and on beaches is bad for all animals. They can become tangled or eat things that harm them. Plastic bags are particularly dangerous, or unsafe, for young greens, which may confuse them for jellyfish.

throwing off the balance between the number of males and females. This imbalance can affect turtle populations when it's time for adults to breed.

Polar ice is melting and causing sea levels to rise. Higher sea levels mean fewer beach areas for greens to use as nesting sites. Warmer ocean waters may also confuse greens about when it's time to migrate to their nesting beaches.

NO DAY AT THE BEACH

Female green sea turtles may nest every two to four years, and they often return to the nesting site where they hatched. A single female will lay between 80 and 200 eggs every few weeks throughout the nesting season.

Sadly, people have greatly harmed many of the nesting sites greens use. Trash and other objects, such as chairs, on a beach may get in a female turtle's way as she comes on shore to lay her eggs. This may cause her to turn around and head back into the ocean.

Beachfront development has reduced the number of peaceful nesting sites for greens. As more beachfront properties are built, beaches become smaller and busier. People may hurt eggs or hatchlings by walking or driving over them.

MARINE ADAPTATIONS

Green turtles are adapted for life in the sea. Their strong flippers help them swim up to 1.4 miles (2.3 km) per hour. They can stay underwater for up to five hours by slowing their heart rate to save oxygen. Their heart may only beat once every nine minutes! Unfortunately, the features that make greens great swimmers cause them to move slowly on land, making them easier targets for predators.

Green turtles may also avoid nesting on beaches where there's lots of noise and human activity. If greens do nest on a busy beach, it's important for people to leave them alone.

In some places, people dig up and eat green sea turtle eggs. On land, racoons, birds, crabs, and dogs will eat both eggs and hatchlings. Sharks and fish will go after hatchlings in the ocean.

After they hatch, it may take up to a week for baby greens to dig out of their nest. They then use moonlight to guide them to the ocean. Other sources of light, such

If hatchlings are lucky enough to reach the ocean, they begin what is known as a "swim frenzy." They swim as fast as they can for 24 to 48 hours until they reach safer, deeper waters.

Green sea turtles play a role in beach ecosystems. Unhatched turtle eggs add important **nutrients** to the sand, which helps plants grow on sand dunes. This creates more stable shorelines. These plants, as well as turtle eggs, also provide food for many beach-dwelling species.

as homes or hotels, near a nesting beach may confuse hatchlings. They may move inland, where they'll often die.

Lights may also confuse female greens coming on shore to lay eggs. Nesting usually occurs at night, but bright lights near a beach might make it look like daytime and females may turn back to the sea.

TURTLE HOSPITALS

Zoos, aquariums, and other organizations around the world have started **rehabilitation** services for sick and injured sea turtles. These are basically turtle hospitals. Sometimes turtles become tangled in fishing lines or other debris. Sometimes they eat trash or are hit by a boat. Turtle hospitals take in these turtles and care for them until they're healthy again. Some turtles require operations.

FIBROPAPILLOMATOSIS

Fibropapillomatosis (FP) is a disease that causes **tumors** to grow on the flippers, neck, and face of many green sea turtles. Large tumors may make it hard for a green to see, eat, swim, or breathe, which may lead to death. Scientists aren't sure what causes FP, but it occurs more in places with increased human activity.

SEA TURTLE HOSPITAL
SEA TURTLE CONSERVATION CENTER
ROYAL THAI NAVY

The goal of turtle rehabilitation is to make sick or injured sea turtles healthy enough to return to their home in the wild. Unfortunately, not all sea turtles heal well enough to be released. These turtles sometimes remain at the facility so their health can be watched and their species can be studied. They're sometimes used to teach the public about the importance of saving sea turtles.

SAVING GREEN SEA TURTLES

In 1978, green sea turtles were listed under the Endangered Species Act (ESA) as threatened or endangered, depending on their location. The ESA makes it illegal to buy, sell, or transport sea turtles and turtle products. In the United States, the U.S. Fish and Wildlife Service is responsible for protecting greens on land, while the National Marine Fisheries Service protects them in the water.

Today, greens continue to be listed differently depending on their location. Different countries and states have different laws in place to protect green turtles, so their populations don't grow evenly everywhere. In some places, greens still don't have any local protection at all. Since greens migrate across the ocean between their feeding and nesting places, the Convention on International Trade in Endangered Species (CITES) was created in 1973 to protect them internationally.

ARCHIE CARR, FATHER OF SEA TURTLE RESEARCH

Archie Carr spent his life studying sea turtles. In 1937, he earned his doctorate in zoology—the study of animals—from the University of Florida. Carr traveled the world learning about different ecosystems. He was most interested in Florida sea turtles and studied them for more than 50 years. He founded several conservation groups and wrote 10 books and more than 120 articles about sea turtles in his lifetime.

Conservation efforts include hatcheries where green sea turtle eggs are kept safe. The baby greens are released into the ocean once they've hatched.

CURRENT STATUS

Besides government agencies, there are many private organizations working to save green sea turtles around the world. These groups educate the public, crack down on illegal activity, and keep nesting beaches clean and peaceful for greens. They also work with government agencies to set up protected lands, such as the Archie Carr National Wildlife Refuge in Florida.

TURTLES RESTING

Stay 15 feet away (including taking pictures)
DO NOT TOUCH TURTLES

カメが休息中
4,5m以内への進入禁止
(写真撮影も含む)

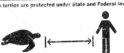

HAWAIIAN GREEN SEA TURTLES

ENJOY THEM FROM A DISTANCE

Sea turtles are protected under State and Federal laws.

PLEASE give turtles space

Sea turtles may come on land to rest.
Please do not disturb or approach turtles.

PLEASE never touch or ride

Sea turtles are wild animals.
Respect and enjoy them from a distance.

PLEASE never feed

Feeding sea turtles

In 2016, the ESA was revised to include 11 distinct populations of green sea turtles. Some populations are growing, but all are still at risk.

As of April 2016, the ESA lists eight populations of green sea turtles as threatened and three as endangered. To guess the number of greens in a population, scientists count the number of nests on important nesting beaches. Using these numbers, scientists believe populations are steady or growing in the Atlantic. However, they believe that, except for the Hawaiian population, populations in much of the Pacific continue to drop.

WHAT CAN YOU DO?

Saving the green sea turtle from extinction is going to take a lot of work, but there are things you can do to help. If you live near a beach where sea turtles nest, turn off, block, or dim the lights around your home at night so nesting females and hatchlings don't get confused. If you visit a beach, especially at night, keep an eye out

Volunteering to clean up a nearby beach is one way to help save green sea turtles. Ask your friends and family to help and tell them why saving greens is important.

for possible nests and hatchlings so you don't walk on them. If you see a green sea turtle, respect its space and don't bother it.

You can help save green turtles even if you don't live near a beach. By using fewer chemicals and reducing the amount of trash you produce, you'll help keep Earth's oceans cleaner and safer for all animals, including greens.

HISTORY OF THE GREEN SEA TURTLE

early 1900s — The turtle-fishing industry brings green sea turtles in Florida close to extinction.

The Brotherhood of the Green Turtle, now called the Sea Turtle Conservancy, is formed. This group partners with the U.S. Navy to create hatch-and-release programs to restore green turtle populations. — **1960s**

1975 — Sea turtles are included in the Convention on International Trade in Endangered Species of Wild Fauna and Flora (CITES) for the first time. Restrictions are placed on the trade of skin, meat, shells, and other parts of green sea turtles.

Green sea turtles are listed under the Endangered Species Act, with populations in certain areas listed as endangered and those in other areas listed as threatened. — **1978**

1981 — CITES prohibits the trade of parts for all types of sea turtles with very limited exceptions.

Rules requiring shrimp trawlers to use turtle excluder devices (TEDs) are put in place. — **1992**

mid-1990s — FP hits its peak so far, affecting approximately 50 percent of green sea turtles.

The coastal waters around Culebra Island, Puerto Rico, are named a critical habitat for green sea turtles. A critical habitat is an area that is essential for conservation. — **1998**

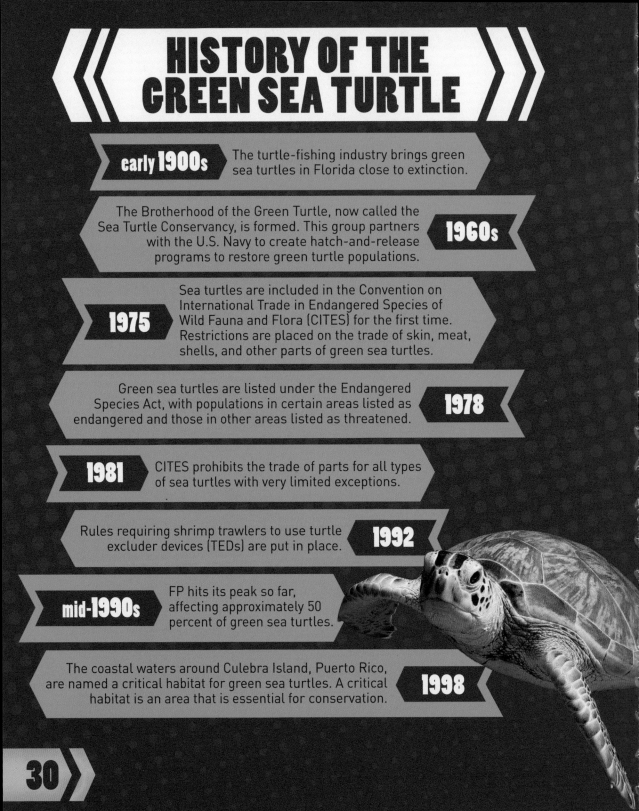

GLOSSARY

adorn: To decorate something.

algae: Plantlike living things without roots or stems that live in water.

decline: To become less in amount.

disaster: Something that happens suddenly and causes much suffering and loss.

ecosystem: A natural community of living and nonliving things.

environmental: Having to do with the natural world.

excluder: Something that keeps someone or something out.

nutrient: Something taken in by a plant or animal that helps it grow and stay healthy.

overexploit: To use a renewable resource to the point where it starts to run out.

rehabilitation: The process of making something healthy again.

tumor: A growth of cells in the body that isn't normal.

INDEX

WEBSITES

Due to the changing nature of Internet links, PowerKids Press has developed an online list of websites related to the subject of this book. This site is updated regularly. Please use this link to access the list: www.powerkidslinks.com/bbe/turtle